People in the Community

Firefighters

Diyan Leake

Heinemann Library
Chicago, Illinois

Customer Service 888-454-2279
Visit our website at www.heinemannraintree.com

Designed by Joanna Hinton-Malivoire and Steve Mead
Printed in China by South China Printing Company Limited

12 11 10 09
10 9 8 7 6 5 4 3 2

The Library of Congress has cataloged the first edition as follows:
Leake, Diyan.
  Firefighters / Diyan Leake.
      p. cm. -- (People in the community)
  Includes bibliographical references and index.
  ISBN-13: 978-1-4329-1189-8 (hbk.)
  ISBN-13: 978-1-4329-1196-6 (pbk.)
  1. Fire fighters--Juvenile literature. 2. Fire extinction--Juvenile literature. I. Title.
  TH9148.L37 2008
  363.37--dc22
                    2007045071

Acknowledgments
The publishers would like to thank the following for permission to reproduce photographs:
©Age Fotostock pp. **4** (Sylvain Gradadam), **6** (Raymond Forbes), **22 (top)** Sylvain Grandadam); ©Alamy pp. **9** (Pictor International/ImageState), **10** (Ton Koene/Picture Contact), **21** (Shout); ©Corbis pp. **8**, **11** (Richard Hutchings); ©Getty Images pp. **7** (Chung Sung-Jun), **12** (Code Red), **13** (Code Red), **14** (Scoopt), **18** (Robyn Beck/AFP), **19** (Joe Raedle), **22 (bottom)** (Code Red); ©iStockphoto (Brandon Clark) p. **15**; ©Landov pp. **16** (Marcus Fuehrer), **17** (Xinhua); ©Redux (Robert Stolarik/The New York Times) p. **20**; ©Shutterstock (Mika Heittola) p. **5**.

Front cover photograph of firefighters trying to quell an oil fire in Alaska, USA, reproduced with permission of ©Age Fotostock (Zuma Press). Back cover photograph reproduced with permission of ©Landov (Marcus Fuehrer).

Every effort has been made to contact copyright holders of any material reproduced in this book. Any omissions will be rectified in subsequent printings if notice is given to the publisher.

Contents

Communities

People live in communities.

People work in communities.

Firefighters in the Community

Firefighters work in communities.

Firefighters help keep people safe.

What Firefighters Do

Firefighters help put out fires.

Firefighters help people escape
from fires.

Where Firefighters Work

Firefighters work at fire stations.

Firefighters sleep at fire stations.

What Firefighters Use

Firefighters use fire engines.

ladder

Fire engines have ladders.

hose

Fire engines have hoses.

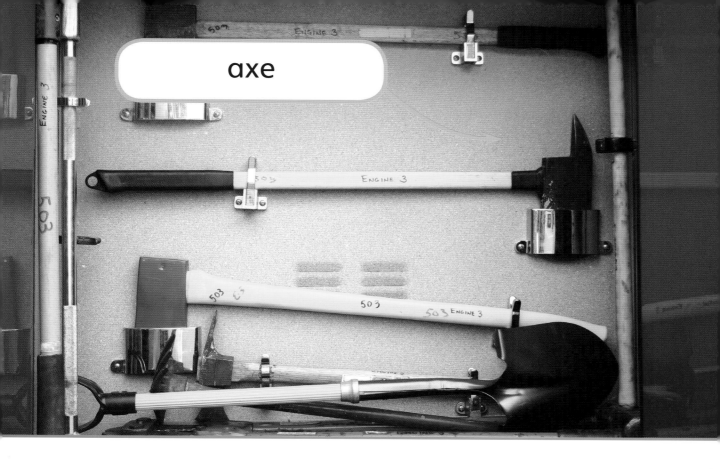

axe

Fire engines have tools.

What Firefighters Wear

Firefighters wear jackets.

Firefighters wear helmets.

Firefighters wear gloves.

Firefighters wear boots.

How Firefighters Help Us

Firefighters help us stay safe.

Firefighters help the community.

Picture Glossary

community group of people living and working in the same area

fire station place where fire engines are kept. Firefighters work and sleep at fire stations.

Index

Note to Parents and Teachers

This series introduces readers to the lives of different community workers, and explains some of the different jobs they perform around the world. Some of the locations featured in this book include Atlanta, GA (page 4); Colwyn Bay, Wales (page 14); Nuremberg, Germany (page 16); Beijing, China (page 17); Los Angeles, CA (page 18), and Queens, NY (page 20).

Discuss with children their experiences with firefighters in the community. Do they know any firefighters? Have they ever visited a fire station? What was it like? Discuss with children why communities need firefighters.

Ask children to look through the book and name some of the tools firefighters use to help them with their job. Give children poster boards and ask them to draw firefighters. Tell them to show the clothes, tools, and vehicles they use to do their job.

The text has been chosen with the advice of a literacy expert to enable beginning readers success while reading independently or with moderate support. You can support children's nonfiction literacy skills by helping them use the table of contents, picture glossary, and index.